Joke Books

More Funny Knock-Knock Jokes

by Erika L. Shores

Consulting Editor: Gail Saunders-Smith, PhD

CAPSTONE PRESS
a capstone imprint

Pebble Books are published by Capstone Press,
1710 Roe Crest Drive, North Mankato, Minnesota 56003.
www.capstonepub.com

Books published by Capstone Press are manufactured with paper
containing at least 10 percent post-consumer waste.

Library of Congress Cataloging-in-Publication Data
Shores, Erika L., 1976–
  More funny knock-knock jokes / by Erika L. Shores.
     p. cm. — (Pebble books. Joke books)
  Includes bibliographical references.
  Summary: "Simple text and color photographs present knock-knock jokes"—
Provided by publisher.
  ISBN 978-1-4296-7564-2 (library binding)
  1. Knock-knock jokes. 2. Wit and humor, Juvenile. I. Title. II. Series.
  PN6231.K55S56 2012
  818'.602—dc23   2011030104

Editorial Credits
Gillia Olson, editor; Gene Bentdahl, designer; Sarah Schuette, studio specialist;
    Marcy Morin, studio scheduler; Kathy McColley, production specialist

Photo Credits
Capstone Studio: Karon Dubke, cover, 4, 6, 8, 10, 12, 16, 18 (boy), 20, 22
iStockphoto: ross1248, 14
Shutterstock: yui, 18 (yard)

Note to Parents and Teachers

The Pebble Jokes set supports English language arts standards related
to reading a wide range of print for personal fulfillment. Early readers
may need assistance to read some of the words and to use the Table of
Contents, Read More, and Internet Sites sections of this book.

Printed in the United States of America in North Mankato, Minnesota.
102011   006405CGS12

Table of Contents

Don't Play with Your Food . . . 5

Furry Fun 11

And Who Are You? 17

Read More 24

Internet Sites. 24

Knock knock.
Who's there?
Lettuce.
Lettuce who?
Lettuce out of here—
it's cold!

Knock knock.
Who's there?
Olive.
Olive who?
Olive across the road.

Knock knock.
Who's there?
Beets
Beets who?
Beets me.

Knock knock.
Who's there?
Lion.
Lion who?
Lion on your doorstep.
Open up!

Knock knock.
Who's there?
Gorilla.
Gorilla who?
Gorilla me a cheese
sandwich, please.

14

Knock knock.
Who's there?
Kanga.
Kanga who?
No, kangaroo!

Knock knock.
Who's there?
Carrie.
Carrie who?
Carrie this, will you?

Knock knock.
Who's there?
Eddie.
Eddie who?
Eddie body home?

Knock knock.
Who's there?
Mikey.
Mikey who?
Mikey won't fit in
the lock.

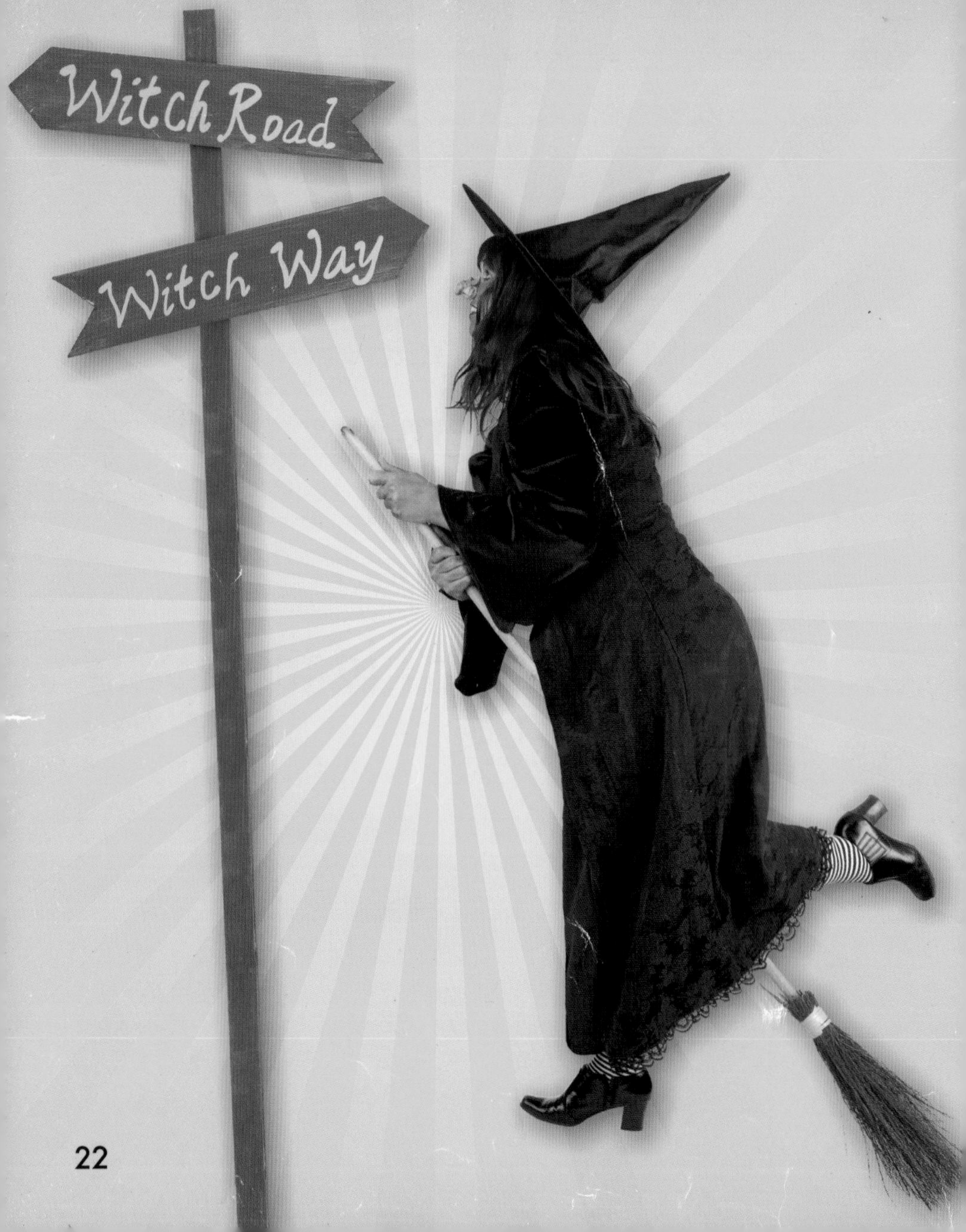
Witch Road
Witch Way

Knock knock.
Who's there?
Witches.
Witches who?
Witches the right
way to go?

Read More

Dahl, Michael. *Knock Your Socks Off: A Book of Knock-Knock Jokes.* Michael Dahl Presents Super Funny Joke Books. Mankato, Minn.: Picture Window Books, 2011.

Rissinger, Matt, and Philip Yates. *Nuttiest Knock-Knocks Ever.* New York: Sterling, 2008.

Winter, Judy A. *Knock-Knock Jokes.* Joke Books. Mankato, Minn.: Capstone Press, 2011.

Internet Sites

FactHound offers a safe, fun way to find Internet sites related to this book. All of the sites on FactHound have been researched by our staff.

Here's all you do:

Visit *www.facthound.com*

Type in this code: 9781429675642

Check out projects, games and lots more at
www.capstonekids.com

Super-cool stuff!

Word Count: 115   Grade: 1
Early-Intervention Level: 20